740

ROCKET PRAYERS

THAT

BREAK WITCHCRAFT EMBARGO

BE SET FREE FROM STAGNANCY AND ANTI-BREAKTHROUGH POWERS

By Tella Olayeri

08023583168

Email; tellaolayeri@gmail.com
Website www.tellaolayeri.com

US Contact
Ruth Jack
14 Milewood Road
Verbank
N.Y.12585
U.S.A. +19176428989

APPRECIATION

I give special appreciation to my wife **MRS NGOZI OLAYER**I for her assistance in ensuring that this book is published and our children that play around us to encourage us day and night.

Also, this manuscript wouldn't have seen the light of the day, if not for the spiritual encouragement I gathered from my father in the Lord, **Dr. D.K. OLUKOYA** who served as spiritual mirror that brightens my hope to explore my calling (Evangelism).

We shall all reap our blessings in heaven but the battle to make heaven is not over, until it is won.

PREFACE

Embargoes are terrible. They are satanically designed to keep good things out of reach, even you merit it. You are denied because you are under spiritual attack. Enemies employ this deadly weapon of frustration to silence your joy and open bank of tears in your eyes. They want tears to flow in your cheeks.

It is time you speak woe to this satanic made tool that keeps victim out Canaan land. Every Red Sea embargo that says you will not occupy your Canaan land is addressed in this book. The wall of Jericho that says you will not capture and disgrace enemies that vow you will not go shall be humiliated and disgrace. Every embargo placed upon your success and breakthrough shall break to pieces.

Brethren, it is high time you rise and speak destruction to satanic embargo troubling you and household, it is time you apply hot acidic and atomic prayers. The book in your hands shall teach you this, so that you experience unprecedented grace and mercy from the throne of God.

GOOD NEWS!!!

My audiobook is now available, to get one visit acx.com and search **"Tella Olayeri."**

Brethren, to be loaded and reloaded visit: *amazon.com/author/tellaolayeri* for a full spiritual sojourn for my books.

Thanks.

PREVIOUS PUBLICATIONS OF THE AUTHOR

1. *Fire for Fire Prayer Book Part 1*
2. *Fire for Fire Prayer Book Part 2*
3. *My Marriage Shall Not Break*
4. *Prayer for Pregnant Women*
5. *Prayer for the Fruit of the Womb*
6. *Children Deliverance*
7. *Prayer for Youths and Teenagers*
8. *Prayer for Singles*
9. *Victory over Satanic House Part 1*
10. *Victory over Satanic House Part 2*
11. *I Shall Excel*
12. *Atomic Prayers that Destroy Witchcraft Powers and Silence Enemies*
13. *Goliath at the Gate of Marriage*
14. *Deliverance from Spirit of Dogs*
15. *Naked Warriors*
16. *Prayer Against Sex in the Dream*
17. *Strange Women! Leave My Husband Alone*
18. *Dangerous Prayer against Strange Women*
19. *630 Acidic Prayer Points*
20. *Power to Retain Job and Excel in Office*
21. *Warfare in the Office*
22. *Command the Year*
23. *Deliverance Prayer for First Born*
24. *800 Deliverance Prayer for First Born Part Two*
25. *Prayer for Good Health and Divine Healing*
26. *Prayer against Untimely Death.*
27. *Dictionary of Dreams*

Table of Contents

CHAPTER 1

PRAYER TO NULLIFY EMBARGO OF DARK CLOUD

Psalm 18 7 -12

7. The earth trembled and quaked, and the foundations of the mountains shook; they trembled because he was angry.

8. Smoke rose from his nostrils; consuming fire came from his mouth, burning coals blazed out of it.

9. He parted the heavens and came down; dark clouds were under his feet.

10. He mounted the cherubim and flew; he soared on the wings of the wind.

11. He made darkness his covering, his canopy around him the dark rain clouds of the sky.

12. Out of the brightness of his presence clouds advanced, with hailstones and bolts of lightning.

Exodus 13:19-20

19. Moses took the bones of Joseph with him because Joseph had made the Israelites swear an oath. He had said, "God will surely come to your aid, and then you must carry my bones up with you from this place."

20. After leaving Sukkoth they camped at Etham on the edge of the desert.

1. O Lord, forgive me, and let embargo of darkness around me break, in the name of Jesus
2. O Lord, forgive me and let every embargo upon my destiny, scatter in the name of Jesus
3. Holy Spirit walk with me and scatter every embargo of darkness upon my life, in the name of Jesus
4. Holy Ghost Fire, consume every dark cloud upon my life in the name of Jesus
5. Holy Ghost Power, scatter every plan of darkness assign to enslave me in the name of Jesus
6. Blood of Jesus, clear every cloud that surrounds my destiny. In the name of Jesus
7. Blood of Jesus speak for me today in the name of Jesus
8. I soak myself with blood of Jesus, against evil cloud, in the name of Jesus
9. O God arise, show your kindness to me, in the name of Jesus
10. O Lord, raise voice of help and deliverance to me, in the name of Jesus.
11. Every ancient battle that vow to see my end, scatter in the name of Jesus
12. Embargo of profitless hard work placed upon me, break in the name of Jesus]

13. Embargo of prayerlessness place upon me, to sponsor cloud upon my life break in the name of Jesus
14. Any power assign stop me from following Jesus, die in the name of Jesus
15. Power of cobweb embargo that keep me in darkness, break and catch fire in the name of Jesus
16. Powers that placed embargo upon me, to turn me to lesser personality, die in the name of Jesus
17. Limiting powers assign to stagnate my destiny, die in the name of Jesus
18. Every embargo placed upon me, to turn my life upside down, your time is up, break, in the name of Jesus
19. Embargo of darkness placed upon my destiny, clear away in the name of Jesus
20. Every cloud that surround my destiny, clear away, in the name of Jesus
21. Every cloud embargo placed upon my greatness, clear away, in the name of Jesus.
22. Wicked negotiation assign to arrest my life, scatter in the name of Jesus
23. Violent storm assign to clear away my destiny, scatter in the name of Jesus

24. Every cloud of darkness battling with my foundation, clear away in the name of Jesus.

25. Any power caging my star with evil cloud, I am not your candidate die in the name of Jesus

26. Today, let the voice that raise Lazarus as in the old, scatter every embargo contending with my glory in the name of Jesus

27. Arrogant power of darkness boasting against my destiny, your time is up, meet your doom in the name of Jesus

28. Every embargo of dark cloud upon my finance, break in the name of Jesus.

29. Every embargo of darkness placed upon my lineage, your time is up, clear away in the name of Jesus

30. Every embargo of sorrow assign to dominate my life, break in the name of Jesus

31. Every dark cloud that held me back from reaching my promised land, scatter, in the name of Jesus

32. Every dark cloud that envelope my breakthrough, clear away in the name of Jesus

33. I command every sword of darkness fashion against me to break in the name of Jesus

34. Partial obedience to word of God keeping me in the cloud, expire in the name of Jesus

35. I command every embargo placed upon my achievement to scatter in the name of Jesus

36. Embargo of witchcraft assign to turn my life miserable break in the name of Jesus

37. Blockers of good things of life, as many as you are against me die, in the name of Jesus

38. O God that answer prayer visit me today in the name of Jesus

39. Where enemy limited me, I shall rise and shine, in the name of Jesus

40. I recover my lost glory kept in the dark cloud of witchcraft power in the name of Jesus

41. My benefits in the hands of the enemy, I recover you in the name of Jesus

42. Anointing the breaks the yoke fall upon me in the name of Jesus

43. My star, be delivered of evil cloud in the name of Jesus

44. Light of God, shine and overpower every dark cloud holding my destiny captive in the name of Jesus

45. My foundation, be delivered of evil cloud in the name of Jesus

CHAPTER 2

I RECEIVE POWER TO BREAK EMBARGO THAT ATTRACTS OPPOSITION.

Isaiah 8:9-10

9. Raise the war cry, you nations, and be shattered! Listen, all you distant lands. Prepare for battle, and be shattered! Prepare for battle, and be shattered!

10. Devise your strategy, but it will be thwarted; propose your plan, but it will not stand, for God is with us.

Exodus 5:6-9

6. That same day Pharaoh gave this order to the slave drivers and overseers in charge of the people:

7. "You are no longer to supply the people with straw for making bricks; let them go and gather their own straw.

8. But require them to make the same number of bricks as before; don't reduce the quota. They are lazy; that is why they are crying out, 'Let us go and sacrifice to our God.'

9. Make the work harder for the people so that they keep working and pay no attention to lies."

1. O Lord, I am on my knee before you for forgiveness and mercy write off my sins, and forgive me by your power in the name of Jesus

2. Power of God to flee sin, fall upon me, in the name of Jesus

3. I thank my God, who forgives and scatter plans of enemy, in the name of Jesus

4. Every lame spirit in me, that advertise my sins for punishment, die, in the name of Jesus

5. I cover myself with blood of Jesus, in the name of Jesus

6. Power in the blood of Jesus, scatter my enemy in the name of Jesus

7. I build wall of protection around me with blood of Jesus

8. Blood of Jesus, flow in my life and strengthen me in the name of Jesus

9. I sprinkle blood of Jesus on embargo that holds me captive, in the name of Jesus

10. O Lord, deliver me from powerful enemies in the name of Jesus

11. Ancient of days arise, fight and defend me in in the battlefield of life in the name of Jesus

12. Family strongman in charge of my case, enough is enough, die in the name of Jesus

13. Evil hands assign to slap me in my sleep, wither, in the name of Jesus

14. Witchcraft embargo placed upon me as a result of evil slap in the spirit, break in the name of Jesus

15. Every embargo place upon me to miss God's deliverance for my life break, in the name of Jesus

16. O Lord, let the wicked perish, in the name of Jesus

17. Every blockage on my way to breakthrough, scatter, in the name of Jesus

18. Evil altar that attract opposition against my prosperity, catch fire and roast to ashes, in the name of Jesus

19. Every embargo that attract opposition to my life as a result of evil food I ate in the dream, break in the name of Jesus

20. Witchcraft pot, cooking my glory to drive helpers away, break, in the name of Jesus

21. Evil padlock fashioned against me to multiply opposition to my life, break in the name of Jesus

22. Wicked embargo placed upon me that refuse me to function in my father's house, break in the name of Jesus

23. Covenant of darkness, operating in my life, break in the name of Jesus

24. Blood of covenant attracting opposition to my life, break in the name of Jesus

25. Embargo that multiply star killers in my life, break in the name of Jesus

26. Any power blocking deliverance of God in my life, die in the name of Jesus

27. Goliath of my father's house, I strike your head with rod of God, run mad and die, in the name of Jesus

28. O Lord, let every enemy of my project be defeated and be disgraced in the name of Jesus

29. Every embargo of opposition for me to live in bitter and sorrow break, in the name of Jesus

30. Embargo of darkness upon my life, break and scatter in the name of Jesus

31. Destiny killers of my father's house opposing my breakthrough die, in the name of Jesus.

32. I command forces of darkness against me to scatter in the name of Jesus

33. Sacrifice of darkness assign to introduce embargo of emptiness in my life, catch fire and roast to ashes in the name of Jesus

34. My pictures in the darkroom of darkness operating negatively against me, I retrieve you by fire, be delivered to me, in the name of Jesus

35. Embargo of evil altar that give opposition power against me, break by fire and roast to ashes, in the name of Jesus

36. Net work of darkness against my life, catch fire and roast to ashes in the name of Jesus

37. Falsehood opposition against my person, scatter, in the name of Jesus

38. Light of God, shine upon me for signs and wonders, in the name of Jesus

39. Powers assign to deny me divine solution to problems, your time is up, die in the name of Jesus

40. Darkness in my life, clear away in the name of Jesus

41. Enemy that rises to kill me, you are a liar, die, in the name of Jesus

42. I will not fear the tens of thousands drawn up against me on every side, but shall wipe them out, in the name of Jesus

43. I receive power to beat my enemy to submission in the name of Jesus

44. Every difficult situation in my life shall bow in the name of Jesus

45. Hence forth, I shall receive divine solution to my problem in the name of Jesus

CHAPTER 3

O LORD BREAK EMBARGO THAT SUPPRESS WISDOM

Psalm 91:11-12

11. For he will command his angels concerning you to guard you in all your ways;

12. They will lift you up in their hands, so that you will not strike your foot against a stone.

2 Samuel 15:31

31. Now David had been told, "Ahithophel is among the conspirators with Absalom." So David prayed, "LORD, turn Ahithophel's counsel into foolishness."

1. I thank you Lord, your power is absolute, in the name of Jesus
2. I thank my God that delivers one from arrow of household wickedness in the name of Jesus
3. I thank my God, He anoints my tongue to prosper, in the name of Jesus
4. O Lord, forgive me and multiply my wisdom, in the name of Jesus
5. Lord Jesus, lay hand of breakthrough on my head, in the name of Jesus

6. Holy Ghost Power, dwell in my life, in the name of Jesus

7. I laminate my brain with blood of Jesus

8. Every blood pollution in my body be neutralized by blood of Jesus

9. Every Satanic poison in my head that causes brain failure, dry up in the name of Jesus

10. Every heaviness in my head, die in the name of Jesus

11. Every instrument of darkness targeted against me die in the name of Jesus.

12. Embargo of darkness that causes setback, in my life break in the name of Jesus

13. Every embargo assign to cause me brain damage, break and scatter in the name of Jesus

14. O Lord, teach me when to be silent, and where to speak, in the name of Jesus

15. Embargo placed upon me that provoke angels of God to anger break, in the name of Jesus

16. Embargo placed upon me from speaking truth, break in the name of Jesus

17. Dark embargo hat build mouth odour, clear away in the name of Jesus

18. Every yoke in my hands assign to stop me from carrying out good thing, break in the name of Jesus

19. Spiritual strongman assign to bind my hand, die in the name of Jesus

20. Agenda of the wicked against my destiny, break and scatter, in the name of Jesus

21. Arrow of the wicked against my destiny, break and scatter, in the name of Jesus

22. Joy killers with wicked intention against me, I command you to scatter, in the name of Jesus

23. Wicked embargo that leads to brain failure, I am not your candidate, scatter in the name of Jesus

24. Dream affliction that multiply embargo of failure, die in the name of Jesus

25. Wicked embargo that attracts vision killers to my life, break in the name of Jesus

26. Every embargo that bring contrary plan for me in the spirit, scatter in the name of Jesus

27. Every embargo assign to erase laughter in my mouth, your time is up break, in the name of Jesus

28. O Lord, let my tongue become instrument of fire, in the name of Jesus

29. Every embargo placed upon my head to turn my brain to brain of animal break and scatter in the name of Jesus

30. O God arise, let me operate in higher realm, in the name of Jesus

31. Embargo of evil clinical prophecy targeted against my brain, break, in the name of Jesus

32. Story of my life, whether you like it or not, change in the name of Jesus

33. O Lord, let me experience divine visitation tonight, in the name of Jesus

34. O Lord, release key of deep wisdom to me in the name of Jesus

35. My wisdom shall not expire in the name of Jesus

36. I begin to shine like shining star because embargo on me is broken, in the name of Jesus

37. O Lord let the grace of my Heavenly Father that makes the day break, make me break new grounds with ease, in the name of Jesus

38. Let the grace of my Heavenly Father that makes the day break, make break new grounds beyond my imagination in the name of Jesus

39. Let the grace and mercy of God, that makes the day break, make me achieve good dreams, in the name of Jesus

40. Let the heavens arise for my sake and expand my wisdom in the name of Jesus

41. Let the heavens support me to harvest good returns in what I do, in the name of Jesus

42. Let the glorious expectation of new things manifest in my life in the name of Jesus

43. Let the Lord make me eat and dine among nobles in the name of Jesus

44. By the power of the Living God, I shall be called upon by kings for consultation in the name of Jesus

45. O Lord, let my wisdom translate to testimonies in the name of Jesus.

CHAPTER 4

O LORD BREAK EVERY EMBARGO THAT KILLS PROSPERITY

Psalm 25:11-13

11. For the sake of your name, LORD, forgive my iniquity, though it is great.

12. Who, then, are those who fear the LORD? He will instruct them in the ways they should choose.

13. They will spend their days in prosperity, and their descendants will inherit the land.

Psalm 91:5-6

5. You will not fear the terror of night, nor the arrow that flies by day,

6. Nor the pestilence that stalks in the darkness, nor the plague that destroys at midday.

1. I thank you Lord for your love and protection over me, in the name of Jesus
2. I thank my God that shall execute judgment against witchcraft activity after my life in the name of Jesus
3. Lord Jesus, forgive me every sin that derail my prosperity, in the name of Jesus

4. Sins that multiply poverty, I do away with you, in the name of Jesus

5. Holy Spirit guide my speech for multiple breakthroughs in the name of Jesus

6. Holy Spirit, flush my destiny of poverty in the name of Jesus

7. Blood of Jesus, surround me and laminate my life against poverty in the name of Jesus

8. I drink blood of Jesus and purge myself of every element of poverty, in the name of Jesus

9. Evil deposit in my prosperity, catch fire and roast to ashes in the name of Jesus

10. Power of fast and pray, fall upon me for multiple breakthrough in the name of Jesus

11. O Lord, plug my destiny to socket of success, in the name of Jesus

12. Failure magnet in my hands, die in the name of Jesus

13. Covenant of darkness with poverty, I break your embargo upon my life in the name of Jesus

14. Every curse pronounced against my prosperity, backfire in the name of Jesus

15. Witchcraft embargo that attracts miracle hijackers to my life break in the name of Jesus

16. Every embargo at the edge of breakthrough, break, in the name of Jesus

17. Satanic vow, that raised embargo to frustrate me will not prosper, break and backfire in the name of Jesus

18. Witchcraft pot cooking my prosperity, break in the name of Jesus

19. Embargo of darkness upon my prosperity break in the name of Jesus

20. Yoke of poverty in my life, break in the name of Jesus

21. Foundational strongman, die with your embargo in the name of Jesus

22. Dark house that held my prosperity, release it now, catch fire and roast to ashes, in the name of Jesus

23. Luggage of embargo in my possession, break, catch fire and roast to ashes in the name of Jesus

24. Evil storm raised against my prosperity, scatter in the name of Jesus

25. Certificate of debt as a result of wicked embargo against my life, catch fire and roast to ashes, in the name of Jesus

26. Satanic maggot in my prosperity, die in the name of Jesus

27. I unplug my life from socket of poverty, in the name of Jesus

28. Anointing of money failure in my life, tonight is your last day, dry up, in the name of Jesus

29. Evil commandment issued against my prosperity, backfire in the name of Jesus.

30. Arrow of darkness fired against my prosperity, backfire in the name of Jesus

31. Embargo in place that give evil command to mislead me break in the name of Jesus

32. Evil veil that covers my face from recognizing opportunities around me catch fire, and roast to ashes, in the name of Jesus

33. Workers of iniquity troubling my soul, die in the name of Jesus

34. Strongman, assign to snatch my bag of glory from me die, in the name of Jesus

35. Strongman that signs my cheque book on my behalf in the spirit, to empty my account, die in the name of Jesus

36. Demonic attachment in my life, catch fire and roast to ashes, in the name of Jesus

37. Owner of evil load, carry your load, in the name of Jesus

38. Every plan of strongman and strongwoman to arrest my finance, scatter in the name of Jesus

39. My hands, reject poverty in the name of Jesus

40. Satanic sacrifice against my prosperity, backfire in the name of Jesus

41. I raise sword of God and scatter enemies of my soul, in the name of Jesus
42. O Lord, let evil agenda against me, scatter, in the name of Jesus
43. O God of Elijah, multiply my miracle and surprise the world, in the name of Jesus
44. Anointing that provoke blessing, fall upon me, in the name of Jesus
45. My hands shall harvest the fruit of my labour, in the name of Jesus
46. By fire by force, I take back everything enemy stole from me, in the name of Jesus
47. My cup of breakthrough full and run over, in the name of Jesus
48. Every good thing I touch shall prosper, in the name of Jesus
49. I execute judgment against witchcraft powers of my father's house, that boast I shall not prosper, in the name of Jesus
50. Henceforth, my life shall be for signs and wonders, in Jesus name I pray. Amen

CHAPTER 5

PRAYER TO NULLIFY DESTRUCTIVE EMBARGO

Leviticus 26:6-8

6. "'I will grant peace in the land, and you will lie down and no one will make you afraid. I will remove wild beasts from the land, and the sword will not pass through your country.

7. You will pursue your enemies, and they will fall by the sword before you.

8. Five of you will chase a hundred, and a hundred of you will chase ten thousand, and your enemies will fall by the sword before you.

Deuteronomy 9:1-3

1. Hear, Israel: You are now about to cross the Jordan to go in and dispossess nations greater and stronger than you, with large cities that have walls up to the sky.

2. The people are strong and tall Anakites! You know about them and have heard it said: "Who can stand up against the Anakites?"

3. But be assured today that the LORD your God is the one who goes across ahead of you like a devouring fire. He will destroy them; he will subdue them before you. And you will drive them out and annihilate them quickly, as the LORD has promised you.

1. I thank you Lord, for nullifying demonic embargo in my life in the name of Jesus
2. I thank my God, for his protection upon my life, in the name of Jesus
3. I thank Jesus, the silencer of my enemy in the name of Jesus
4. Lord Jesus, forgive me and elevate me tonight in the name of Jesus
5. I shall enjoy total divine forgiveness tonight in the name of Jesus
6. Holy Ghost Power, fight on my behalf tonight in the name of Jesus
7. Holy Spirit, fill me with power that overturn works of darkness, in the name of Jesus
8. Blood of Jesus, heal me of evil attack in the name of Jesus
9. I laminate my life with blood of Jesus against evil arrow in the name of Jesus.
10. I drink blood of Jesus, and purge myself of impurity in the name of Jesus
11. Powers that boast prayer shall not solve my problem, you are a liar, my God shall do it, in the name of Jesus
12. Destructive embargo of debt in my life, break and scatter in the name of Jesus

13. O Lord, let old battles in my family line, scatter and die in the name of Jesus

14. O Lord, I command anointing that breaks power of disfavour fall upon me in the name of Jesus

15. Tonight, I command anointing that breaks power of failure to fall upon me in the name of Jesus

16. Embargo of destructive power against academic glory in my family, break in the name of Jesus

17. Embargo of joblessness in my lineage break in the name of Jesus

18. Power that cause untimely death my life is not your candidate, die in the name of Jesus

19. Embargo against my survival break in the name of Jesus

20. Embargo against my success, break in the name of Jesus

21. Every embargo placed upon my marriage, I command you to break in the name of Jesus

22. Embargo of confusion placed upon my life, break in the name of Jesus

23. Arrow of sickness fired into my life to cause embargo of stagnancy in my life, backfire to your sender in the name of Jesus

24. I command every arrow of seeing but not attaining it fired into my life to backfire to the sender in the name of Jesus
25. Every embargo of bewitchment upon my destiny, break in the name of Jesus
26. Powers assign to gradually dispossess me of my wealth die in the name of Jesus
27. Spirit of aimlessness in my life, die in the name of Jesus
28. Destructive spirit assign to cause sorrow in my life, die in the name of Jesus
29. Enemy assign to break my teeth in the spirit, meet double tragedy in the name of Jesus
30. Powers assign to strike me on the jaw, today is your last day, die in the name of Jesus
31. Embargo of wasters upon my life, to waste me before my time, break, in the name of Jesus
32. Embargo placed upon me to deny me escape from distress and calamity, break in the name of Jesus
33. Any power sponsoring problems in my life, today is you last day die, in the name of Jesus
34. Destructive embargo on my eyes, to destroy my sight and inner vision, break and scatter, in the name of Jesus
35. Every embargo of unexplainable load upon my head, scatter in the name of Jesus

36. Destructive arrows that cause fear in my life, backfire to your sender in the name of Jesus

37. Arrow of debt assign to keep me in the valley, backfire to your sender in the name of Jesus

38. Destructive embargo placed on my ear, break in the name of Jesus

39. Witchcraft powers after my destiny, die, in the name of Jesus

40. O Lord, let my helpers rejoice to help me, in the name of Jesus

41. My body is delivered of demonic attack, in the name of Jesus

42. Every bar of darkness fashioned against me, break and scatter in the name of Jesus

43. Instrument of darkness fashion against my breakthrough, catch fire and roast to ashes, in the name of Jesus

44. O Lord, catapult me to next level of greatness, in the name of Jesus

45. Voice of darkness shall expire without effect in my life, in the name of Jesus.

CHAPTER 6

SCATTERING THE EMBARGO THAT PLACE DESTINY IN THE VALLEY

1 Samuel 2:6-8

6. "The LORD brings death and makes alive; he brings down to the grave and raises up.

7. The LORD sends poverty and wealth; he humbles and he exalts.

8. He raises the poor from the dust and lifts the needy from the ash heap; he seats them with princes and has them inherit a throne of honor. "For the foundations of the earth are the LORD's; on them he has set the world.

Psalm 18:17-19

17. He rescued me from my powerful enemy, from my foes, who were too strong for me.

18. They confronted me in the day of my disaster, but the LORD was my support.

19. He brought me out into a spacious place; he rescued me because he delighted in me.

1. I thank my God that keeps me in perfect peace, in the name of Jesus

2. I thank my Lord that rescue my destiny from evil hands, in the name of Jesus

3. Thank you Lord for removing every embargo enemy placed on me, in the name of Jesus

4. Lord Jesus, I plead for mercy, forgive me the sins that makes me stink before you in the name of Jesus

5. I cry to my God for mercy, and he heard me, in the name of Jesus

6. Holy Ghost Power, touch my life for signs and wonders in the name of Jesus

7. I cover myself with blood of Jesus and regain freedom from the valley in the name of Jesus

8. I sprinkle blood of Jesus on my foundation, to resurrect and bring multiple breakthrough in the name of Jesus

9. Blood of Jesus, mix with my blood and lift me out of the valley, in the name of Jesus

10. Wicked embargo assign to uproot my tree of life planted by streams of water, break and scatter, in the name of Jesus

11. Garment of darkness that leads me to valley of life, catch fire and roast to ashes in the name of Jesus

12. Powers behind my problem, die, in the name of Jesus

13. My prayer, draw attention of Jesus to me, in the name of Jesus

14. Powers killing me small, small, bit by bit, die in the name of Jesus

15. Every embargo placed upon the fruitlessness of my life break, in the name of Jesus

16. Ancient gate standing between me and my breakthrough, I pull you down, in the name of Jesus.

17. Environmental embargo monitoring me for evil, beak in the name of Jesus

18. Sudden anger in me that chase people away from me, expire in the name of Jesus

19. Evil mark in my body, chasing helpers away, expire in the name of Jesus

20. Every embargo placed upon me in my sleep, break, in the name of Jesus

21. Embargo assign to destroy me, break, in the name of Jesus

22. Every enchantment against my life, backfire, in the name of Jesus

23. Embargo of Satanic prophets with evil command against my destiny, break in the name of Jesus

24. My garment in the altar of darkness that makes me poor, catch fire and roast to ashes, in the name of Jesus

25. Every embargo that program battle into my life, break in the name of Jesus
26. Every embargo that troubles destiny, my life is not your candidate, break in the name of Jesus
27. My stubborn pursuers, be wasted, in the name of Jesus
28. Evil deposit in my life that placed embargo of stagnation in my life, come out and die, in the name of Jesus
29. Every embargo placed on my health so that I remain in the valley break in the name of Jesus
30. Every embargo placed on my career and ministry so that I remain in the valley, break in the name of Jesus
31. Every embargo placed on my marriage so that my home should scatter, you are a liar, break, in the name of Jesus
32. Every embargo placed on my wealth so that I remain poor, I rebuke you, break, in the name of Jesus
33. Every poor situation assign to consume me, scatter in the name of Jesus
34. I command every situation that open way to the valley to expire in the name of Jesus
35. Every power behind my problem, I command you to die in the name of Jesus

36. Every strongman and woman in charge of my case, die in the name of Jesus
37. Witchcraft market in charge of my destiny, catch fire and roast to ashes in the name of Jesus
38. Any power making it difficult for me to excel in life, die in the name of Jesus
39. Spiritual rags in my body, I pull you off, in the name of Jesus
40. My life in the valley, receive divine solution, in the name of Jesus
41. I anchor my life to Jesus and shall be permanent, in the name of Jesus
42. Wealth and riches are my portion in the name of Jesus
43. I recover my belongings from valley of darkness, in the name of Jesus
44. By word of prophecy, I shall not be a candidate of the valley, in the name of Jesus
45. By word of prophecy, every dark judgment against me is nullified, in the name of Jesus

CHAPTER 7

O LORD BREAK EMBARGO PLACED UPON MY WEALTH

Deuteronomy 15:6-8

6. For the LORD your God will bless you as he has promised, and you will lend to many nations but will borrow from none. You will rule over many nations but none will rule over you.

7. If anyone is poor among your fellow Israelites in any of the towns of the land the LORD your God is giving you, do not be hardhearted or tightfisted toward them.

8. Rather, be openhanded and freely lend them whatever they need.

Psalm 92:12-14

12. The righteous will flourish like a palm tree, they will grow like a cedar of Lebanon;

13. planted in the house of the LORD, they will flourish in the courts of our God.

14. They will still bear fruit in old age, they will stay fresh and green.

1. I thank you O Lord for making every evil arrow fired against me backfire to the sender in the name of Jesus

2. I thank you Lord, for disengaging Satanic network against my finance in the name of Jesus

3. O Lord forgive me every sin that will make you look elsewhere, in the name of Jesus

4. I wash my hands from sins that makes me stink before my creator in the name of Jesus

5. Holy Ghost Power, destroy every negative embargo troubling my destiny, in the name of Jesus

6. I drink blood of Jesus to neutralize and destroy evil deposit in my body in the name of Jesus

7. I cover myself with blood of Jesus and receive divine strength in the name of Jesus

8. Blood of Jesus, join together my fragmented finance for breakthrough explosion, in the name of Jesus

9. O Lord, deliver me from my powerful enemy in the name of Jesus

10. Every embargo of "start a project but shall not finish" placed on me, in the name of Jesus

11. Every problem designed to scatter my finance, die in the name of Jesus

12. Every embargo of darkness upon my life, to night is your last day, break in the name of Jesus

13. Witchcraft agenda against my finance, scatter in the name of Jesus
14. I command every embargo as a result of enchantment against me to scatter in the name of Jesus
15. Embargo of power of cobwebs against my finance scatter, in the name of Jesus
16. Let cobweb of darkness upon my life, catch fire and roast to ashes, in the name of Jesus
17. Every dark cobweb in my hands, assign to cause poverty in my life, catch fire and roast to ashes, in the name of Jesus
18. Every cobweb of darkness, that covers my business, catch fire and roast to ashes in the name of Jesus
19. Fire of deliverance, enter my foundation and break every embargo placed upon my wealth in the name of Jesus
20. Every embargo that attracts rejection to my life, break, in the name of Jesus
21. Every embargo that attracts failure into my career, break and scatter in the name of Jesus
22. Embargo of joblessness upon my life, scatter in the name of Jesus
23. Powers assign to dry source of my income, die in the name of Jesus

24. Spirit of sickness planted in my life, to drain my account die in the name of Jesus
25. I command every bewitchment against my account to die, in the name of Jesus
26. Embargo of sorrow upon my life scatter in the name of Jesus
27. O Lord, let every evil load designed for me catch fire in the name of Jesus
28. Embargo of debt holding me captive, break in the name of Jesus
29. I command every embargo placed upon the source of my wealth to break in the name of Jesus
30. Spirit of poverty monitoring me about, die in the name of Jesus
31. Embargo of poverty placed upon me in the spirit, break in the name of Jesus
32. O Lord, let any power assign to scatter my home, be put to disgrace, in the name of Jesus
33. Power of confusion upon my life, die in the name of Jesus
34. I break embargo of promise and fail, placed upon me in the name of Jesus.
35. I break embargo of see but not attain placed upon me, in the name of Jesus
36. Embargo of failure, placed upon my career, scatter in the name of Jesus

37. I command every organized battle against my life to scatter, in the name of Jesus

38. I command my glory in the captivity of darkness, to escape and locate me in the name of Jesus

39. Every embargo as a result of my picture used for evil purpose, scatter in the name of Jesus

40. Let every foundation of poverty in my family line, die in the name of Jesus

41. Embargo of demotion in my life, scatter in the name of Jesus

42. My star, arise and shine, in the name of Jesus

43. Miracles and testimony, be my portion in the name of Jesus

44. Rain of miracle baptize my source of income in the name of Jesus

45. Resurrection power of God, wake my wealth to life, in the name of Jesus

CHAPTER 8

O LORD SCATTER EVERY EMBARGO PLACED UPON MY MARRIAGE

Psalm 128:5-6

5. May the LORD bless you from Zion; may you see the prosperity of Jerusalem all the days of your life.

6. May you live to see your children's children peace be on Israel.

Isaiah 54:14-15

14. In righteousness you will be established: Tyranny will be far from you; you will have nothing to fear. Terror will be far removed; it will not come near you.

15. If anyone does attack you, it will not be my doing; whoever attacks you will surrender to you.

1. I thank you Lord for you shall lift and scatter every embargo place upon my marriage, in the name of Jesus
2. I thank you Lord, for you shall silence enemies that say I will not laugh in my marriage, in the name of Jesus.
3. Lord Jesus, forgive me and my spouse, and take our family to greater height in the name of Jesus

4. O Lord, let your forgiveness upon my family be total, in the name of Jesus

5. Holy Spirit, sow seed of love and happiness in my marriage in the name of Jesus

6. Holy Ghost Power, strengthen my marriage, in the name of Jesus

7. I cover everything that concerns my marriage with blood f Jesus, in the name of Jesus

8. Blood of Jesus, encircle my marriage for favour and greatness, in the name of Jesus

9. Every enemy of my marriage be disgraced in the name of Jesus

10. Every arrow in my body waiting to manifest to scatter my marriage backfire, in the name of Jesus

11. Principalities and powers assign to scatter my marriage, your time is up, die, in the name of Jesus

12. I command every challenge in my marriage to expire, in the name of Jesus

13. Every dark judge hired to place embargo upon my marriage, die in the name of Jesus

14. Court of darkness raised against my marriage, scatter and catch fire, in the name of Jesus

15. Owner of evil load, carry your load, in the name of Jesus

16. Let every enemy of my marriage receive arrow of madness, in the name of Jesus
17. I cut off hands of enemies against my marriage, in the name of Jesus
18. I command powers that punish my parents now waging war against me to die in the name of Jesus
19. Powers attacking my joy, your end has come, die, in the name of Jesus
20. Powers that sit on my marital breakthrough, die in the name of Jesus
21. Powers that vow their embargo shall work against my marriage, die, in the name of Jesus
22. Powers stealing from my marriage, die in the name of Jesus
23. Powers assign to suck the honey of my marriage, die, in the name of Jesus
24. Doors of darkness enemy lock against my marriage, break, open in the name of Jesus
25. Every embargo placed on my marriage not to work, scatter in the name of Jesus
26. Every embargo placed upon my spouse, scatter, in the name of Jesus
27. Every embargo placed upon my children, break and scatter, in the name of Jesus

28. Every embargo placed upon the house we live, troubling my marriage, break and scatter, in the name of Jesus
29. Every limitation imposed by power of darkness upon my breakthrough break in the name of Jesus
30. Evil power assign to place embargo of frustration upon me, die, in the name of Jesus
31. Hardship that arise to bring me down as a result of evil embargo die, in the name of Jesus
32. Hardship that slows down progress as a result of dark embargo, die, in the name of Jesus
33. Hardship that makes enemy laugh at me scatter in the name of Jesus
34. Territorial witchcraft embargo upon my life, break, in the name of Jesus
35. Territorial bondage that held me captive, break in the name of Jesus
36. I command every embargo that turns helpers away to scatter in the name of Jesus
37. I command every embargo placed on me that attract enemy to scatter in the name of Jesus
38. Every embargo placed on me that make helpers walk away from me break in the name of Jesus.
39. Every embargo assign to uproot me from my place of breakthrough, break in the name of Jesus

40. Every embargo placed on my hand not to prosper, tonight is your last day, break in the name of Jesus

41. I command every embargo placed on me to lose my yields in my season of breakthrough to break in the name of Jesus

42. Any power assign to waste my resources be wasted in the name of Jesus

43. Health crisis embargo upon my life, expire in the name of Jesus

44. Today is my day, I walk away from bus stop of stagnancy to accelerated breakthroughs, in the name of Jesus

45. I claim what I lost as a result of evil embargo in the name of Jesus

46. My wealth wherever you are, appear and locate me in the name of Jesus

47. Anointing of success locate me in the name of Jesus

48. This night, my God shall bless me beyond expectation in the name of Jesus

49. Favour of God, locate me by fire in the name of Jesus

50. Henceforth, helpers will rejoice to help me in the name of Jesus

CHAPTER 9

LET EVERY EMBARGO AGAISNT LONG LIFE BREAK

Numbers 14:17-19

17. "Now may the Lord's strength be displayed, just as you have declared:

18. 'The LORD is slow to anger, abounding in love and forgiving sin and rebellion. Yet he does not leave the guilty unpunished; he punishes the children for the sin of the parents to the third and fourth generation.'

19. In accordance with your great love, forgive the sin of these people, just as you have pardoned them from the time they left Egypt until now."

1 Corinthians 15:54-55

54. When the perishable has been clothed with the imperishable, and the mortal with immortality, then the saying that is written will come true: "Death has been swallowed up in victory."

55. "Where, O death, is your victory? Where, O death, is your sting?"

1. I thank my God, for His eyes that do not sleep nor slumber watch over me, in the name of Jesus

2. I thank my God, that breaks wicked embargo against long life, in the name of Jesus

3. Lord Jesus, protect me from demonic powers assign to cut my life short, in the name of Jesus

4. Holy Spirit, silence destiny killers assign to waste my life in the name of Jesus

5. Foundational battles assign to waste my life, scatter in the name of Jesus

6. Pollution in my blood clear away in the name of Jesus

7. Evil deposit in my body today is your expiring day, die in the name of Jesus

8. Lord Jesus, purify my blood by your power in the name of Jesus

9. O Lord, give me relief from distress, in the name of Jesus

10. O Lord let the voice that raise up Lazarus, roar and scatter embargo of darkness placed upon my existence, in the name of Jesus

11. Let embargo of Haman upon me, break in the name of Jesus

12. I command every embargo of hardship placed upon me to break in the name of Jesus

13. I command power assign to kill profitable opportunity in my life to die, in the name of Jesus

14. Embargo that kills success and cause problem in my life, break and scatter in the name of Jesus
15. Embargo that kills anointing in my life, break in the name of Jesus
16. Incantation of bewitchment against my life, backfire in the name of Jesus
17. I command rock of ages to crush arrogant powers, pursuing my life, in the name of Jesus
18. Let power of the shadow of death after my life, die in the name of Jesus
19. I command every battle assign to swallow my life, to scatter in the name of Jesus
20. Evil association laboring hard to destroy me, scatter, in the name of Jesus
21. I shall not die in the camp of my enemy, in the name of Jesus
22. Every agent of the grave, appearing in my life, die, in the name of Jesus
23. Any agent of darkness, using the night to trouble me, die in the name of Jesus
24. Any power using evil pot to fight my destiny your time is up, die in the name of Jesus
25. Any power assign to scatter my plan the hand of the Lord is against you, die in the name of Jesus

26. Program of failure for my life, scatter in the name of Jesus

27. Agent of death, after my glory, your time is up, die in the name of Jesus.

28. Trap of death, on my way, catch fire and roast to ashes in the name of Jesus

29. Enemies that want tears to flow down my cheek like river, die in the name of Jesus

30. Witchcraft agenda for my life, scatter in the name of Jesus

31. Every opposition against my destiny, scatter in the name of Jesus

32. Opportunity wasters in the corridor of my life, die in the name of Jesus

33. Every obstacle to my testimony, expire, in the name of Jesus

34. Powers assign to inject me in the spirit, die in the name of Jesus

35. Strange sickness keeping me in the valley, seize to operate in my life, in the name of Jesus

36. Evil label in my body, caused by evil embargo, expire in the name of Jesus

37. Every curse troubling my life, as a result of embargo of darkness, break in the name of Jesus

38. Powers of darkness operating in my life, die in the name of Jesus

39. O Lord, pour fresh anointing into my life, in the name of Jesus
40. Every long time and short time sickness in my body, receive healing in the name of Jesus
41. Witchcraft sickness in my body, receive healing in the name of Jesus
42. Lord Jesus, don't leave me alone, remember me and redeem me in the name of Jesus
43. O Lord, let your healing power begin to operate in my life, in the name of Jesus
44. Fire of God, refine my life, in the name of Jesus
45. Hallelujah, I am delivered of witchcraft attack in the name of Jesus

CHAPTER 10

SCATTERING EMBARGO RAISED BY SPIRIT SPOUSE

Judges 14:16-17

16. Then Samson's wife threw herself on him, sobbing, "You hate me! You don't really love me. You've given my people a riddle, but you haven't told me the answer." "I haven't even explained it to my father or mother," he replied, "so why should I explain it to you?"

17. She cried the whole seven days of the feast. So on the seventh day he finally told her, because she continued to press him. She in turn explained the riddle to her people.

Psalm 29:2-4

2. Ascribe to the LORD the glory due his name; worship the LORD in the splendor of his holiness.

3. The voice of the LORD is over the waters; the God of glory thunders, the LORD thunders over the mighty waters.

4. The voice of the LORD is powerful; the voice of the LORD is majestic.

1. I thank you Lord for your love for me, in the name of Jesus

2. I thank you Lord for your protection of my life in the name of Jesus

3. I thank you Lord that you will silence spirit spouse troubling my life, in the name of Jesus

4. O Lord, forgive me every sin that makes me stink before you in the name of Jesus

5. Lord Jesus, lay your hand of forgiveness upon me, in the name of Jesus

6. Holy Ghost Fire, fight for me tonight, in the name of Jesus

7. I cover myself with blood of Jesus against intimidation of spirit spouse in the name of Jesus

8. I sprinkle blood of Jesus on my bed to stop evil visit of spirit spouse in my life in the name of Jesus

9. I sprinkle blood of Jesus on my door post against visit of spirit spouse in my home, in the name of Jesus

10. Holy Spirit Divine, protect me from spirit spouse that troubles me, in the name of Jesus

11. Embargo of no marriage controlling my life, break in the name of Jesus

12. I command every embargo that attracts spirit spouse to me to break in the name of Jesus

13. Let every strange ring that attracts sprit spouse to me, catch fire and roast to ashes in the name of Jesus

14. Embargo as a result of strange ring of spirit spouse break, in the name of Jesus

15. Embargo as a result of strange garment of spirit spouse break, in the name of Jesus

16. I gather every strange material in my possession attracting spirit spouse and set it ablaze in the name of Jesus

17. Embargo as a result of spirit spouse intimidation break, in the name of Jesus

18. I command fire of God to surround me twenty four hours every day against spirit spouse intimidation in the name of Jesus

19. O Lord, let spirit spouse after my life die, in the name of Jesus

20. I command fire of God to consume every dark food prepared for me in the spirit in the name of Jesus

21. Hardship as a result of spirit spouse, expire in the name of Jesus

22. Embargo of spirit spouse in my life that turn helpers away from me, break in the name of Jesus

23. Embargo of spirit spouse in my life, that placed me in the valley of life, break in the name of Jesus

24. Embargo of spirit spouse in my life, not to walk in the counsel of God, break in the name of Jesus

25. Every embargo placed on my marriage to scatter, break in the name of Jesus

26. Every embargo placed on me to run at loss, break in the name of Jesus

27. I command every embargo assign to turn my life upside down to scatter, in the name of Jesus

28. Powers assign to waste my life, be wasted in the name of Jesus

29. Every enemy of good project in my life, die in the name of Jesus.

30. Ancient of days, arise for my sake and silence spirit spouse troubling my life, in the name of Jesus

31. Embargo of cobweb placed upon me by spirit spouse break and catch fire in the name of Jesus

32. Embargo of darkness placed upon me to turn me to lesser personality, break, in the name of Jesus

33. Embargo of stagnancy in my life, break in the name of Jesus

34. Every limitation in my destiny as a result of spirit spouse attack, scatter in the name of Jesus.

35. Every covenant with spirit spouse break in the name of Jesus

36. Let enemies of my soul be dashed to pieces like pottery in the name of Jesus

37. Dark powers drawn up against me scatter in the name of Jesus

38. Every embargo created so that I may not lift up my head, break in the name of Jesus

39. Marital crisis in my life, seize, in the name of Jesus

40. O Lord, deliver me from the captivity of spirit spouse, in the name of Jesus

41. O Lord, let every spirit spouse embargo upon me break, in the name of Jesus

42. My body is delivered of spirit spouse in the name of Jesus

43. Every attack of my peace is over in the name of Jesus

44. Henceforth, light of God shall separate me from spirit spouse in the name of Jesus

45. I am delivered of spirit spouse molestation, in the name of Jesus.

CHAPTER 11

O LORD BREAK EMBARGO OF EVIL GANG UP AND CONSPIRACY

Numbers 16:1-3

1. Korah son of Izhar, the son of Kohath, the son of Levi, and certain ReubenitesDathan and Abiram, sons of Eliab, and On son of Pelethbecame insolent

2. and rose up against Moses. With them were 250 Israelite men, well-known community leaders who had been appointed members of the council.

3. They came as a group to oppose Moses and Aaron and said to them, "You have gone too far! The whole community is holy, every one of them, and the LORD is with them. Why then do you set yourselves above the LORD's assembly?"

Psalm 18:37-42

37. I pursued my enemies and overtook them; I did not turn back till they were destroyed.

38. I crushed them so that they could not rise; they fell beneath my feet.

39. You armed me with strength for battle; you humbled my adversaries before me.

40. You made my enemies turn their backs in flight, and I destroyed my foes.

41. They cried for help, but there was no one to save them to the LORD, but he did not answer.

42. I beat them as fine as windblown dust; I trampled them like mud in the streets.

1. I thank you Lord, for you shall scatter every gang up against me in the name of Jesus
2. I thank you Lord for your protection upon my life, in the name of Jesus
3. Lord Jesus have mercy upon me and let my enemy bow, in the name of Jesus
4. O Lord, forgive me so that enemy will not have upper hand in my life in the name of Jesus
5. Holy Spirit, strengthen me beyond human imagination, in the name of Jesus
6. I cover myself with blood of Jesus against powers of darkness in the name of Jesus
7. I drink blood of Jesus, and purge myself of evil deposit in the name of Jesus
8. I spray blood of Jesus against my enemies, they scatter and shall not re-unite, in the name of Jesus
9. Blood of Jesus, break wicked agenda for my life, in the name of Jesus
10. Unrepentant opposition against me, scatter in the name of Jesus

11. Every wickedness of the wicked against me, scatter in the name of Jesus.
12. Every embargo of failure placed upon me, break in the name of Jesus
13. I command every gang up against anointing of God upon me in the name of Jesus
14. I command evil gang up that wants me to drink from cup of sorrow to scatter in the name of Jesus
15. Enemies of my soul, run mad and find no bearing to locate me in the name of Jesus
16. Wicked chains organized for me by evil powers catch fire and roast to ashes, in the name of Jesus
17. O Lord let embargo of stagnancy of wicked conspirators against me scatter in the name of Jesus.
18. I command arrow of God to scatter every gang up aim to put me in hopeless situation, in the name of Jesus
19. Embargo that bring hatred to life, scatter in the name of Jesus
20. Embargo of disaster organized for me in the spirit, break in the name of Jesus
21. Embargo of misfortune placed upon me in the spirit, break in the name of Jesus

22. I command arrow of God to scatter evil gathering against my soul, in the name of Jesus

23. I command thunder fire of God to scatter wicked embargo placed on my wealth, in the name of Jesus

24. Witchcraft embargo placed upon my wealth by conspirators of the dark scatter in the name of Jesus

25. Wicked embargo aimed to scatter my marriage, break in the name of Jesus

26. Satanic conspiracy to destroy agenda of God for my life, scatter in the name of Jesus

27. Conspiracy embargo organized to sink my destiny, break and scatter, in the name of Jesus

28. Powers that conspire to disgrace me, die in the name of Jesus

29. Those whose throat is an open grave to swallow my joy, die in the name of Jesus

30. Those whose throat is an open grave to swallow my wealth, meet double failure in the name of Jesus

31. Those who speak deceit to destroy me be disgraced in the name of Jesus

32. Those that rebel against God in order to destroy me, today is your last day, die in the name of Jesus

33. Owner of evil load, carry your load, in the name of Jesus

34. I decree, let every power that journey with me in other to destroy me die, in the name of Jesus

35. Inherited dark powers troubling my life, die, in the name of Jesus

36. Destiny wasters waiting at point of celebration in other to scatter it, die in the name of Jesus

37. Where enemy tied me, O Lord, untie me and set me free, in the name of Jesus

38. Thou sun of righteousness arise, fight my battle for me, in the name of Jesus

39. Every concluded work of Satan for my life, I cancel you, in the name of Jesus

40. Let the wicked fall into the pit they dug for me, in the name of Jesus

41. Even I sow in tears, I will reap with songs of joy, in the name of Jesus

42. Any power that shot me in the spirit, let the bullet reverse and kill you in the name of Jesus

43. O Lord, make me great as I take refuge in you, in the name of Jesus

44. O Lord spread your protection on me, in the name of Jesus

45. O Lord, make me equation enemy cannot solve or detect in the name of Jesus

46. O Lord, reveal secret of greatness to me, in the name of Jesus

47. Beautiful testimony, locate me by fire, in the name of Jesus

48. Wherever my greatness is hidden, I command it to come out and locate me, in the name of Jesus

49. Anywhere I step, I shall possess, in the name of Jesus

50. My destiny is healed, my foundation is healed, in the name of Jesus.

CHAPTER 12

PRAYER TO BREAK EMBARGO OF HOUSEHOLD WICKEDNESS

Colossians 2:14-15

14. having canceled the charge of our legal indebtedness, which stood against us and condemned us; he has taken it away, nailing it to the cross.

15. And having disarmed the powers and authorities, he made a public spectacle of them, triumphing over them by the cross.

Genesis 37:26-28

26. Judah said to his brothers, "What will we gain if we kill our brother and cover up his blood?

27. Come, let's sell him to the Ishmaelites and not lay our hands on him; after all, he is our brother, our own flesh and blood." His brothers agreed.

28. So when the Midianite merchants came by, his brothers pulled Joseph up out of the cistern and sold him for twenty shekels of silver to the Ishmaelites, who took him to Egypt.

1. I thank you Lord, for you shall silence the wicked in my father's house in the name of Jesus

2. I thank you Lord, for my enemies shall surrender at the mention of your name, in the name of Jesus

3. O Lord, show me mercy, don't allow household wickedness, swallow my glory in the name of Jesus

4. With mercy O Lord, touch my life for signs and wonders, in the name of Jesus

5. Holy Spirit, guide my step wherever I go, in the name of Jesus

6. Holy Spirit Divine fight my battle for me, in the name of Jesus

7. I cover myself with blood of Jesus, and march forward as soldier of Christ in the name of Jesus

8. I drink blood of Jesus, to purify my system and purge evil deposit in my life in the name of Jesus

9. Holy Spirit work miracles in my life, in the name of Jesus

10. O God of power, fill me with power, in the name of Jesus

11. Satanic driver in charge of my destiny, die in the name of Jesus

12. Every power assign to keep me in the valley, die in the name of Jesus

13. Ancestral cage of my father's house, catch fire and roast to ashes in the name of Jesus

14. Embargo of evil padlock fashioned against me, break in the name of Jesus

15. Embargo of satanic operation in my father's house against my destiny, break, in the name of Jesus.

16. Wicked household rope tied round me to stagnate my life, break in the name of Jesus

17. Witch doctor hired to terminate my life, die in the name of Jesus

18. Witchcraft agenda for my life, scatter in the name of Jesus

19. Embargo of curses and spells pronounced against me, break in the name of Jesus

20. Ancestral cage of my father's house that place embargo upon me, break, scatter and catch fire in the name of Jesus

21. Armour of wickedness fashion against me, catch fire, and roast to ashes, in the name of Jesus

22. Root of sickness, as a result of household attack, wither and dry up , in the name of Jesus.

23. Embargo as a result of satanic prophecy against my life, break in the name of Jesus

24. Idolatry food of my father's house that place embargo on my destiny, expire in the name of Jesus

25. Arrow of paralysis fired against me, backfire in the name of Jesus

26. Household witchcraft injection applied in my body, expire tonight in the name of Jesus

27. Let embargo of sudden death placed upon me by household wickedness scatter, in the name of Jesus

28. Every embargo of household wickedness to make me cry, scatter in the name of Jesus

29. I command attacks on my peace to scatter in the name of Jesus

30. Wicked strongman that appear in my dream in other to destroy me, die in the name of Jesus

31. Lion of darkness, assign to devour me, die in the name of Jesus

32. Serpents in my dream, die in the name of Jesus

33. Any power of my father's house using my glory to shine, die in the name of Jesus

34. Embargo that brings anguish today is your last day, break in the name of Jesus.

35. Embargo of agony upon my life break, in the name of Jesus.

36. Every embargo placed upon my unbroken area, so that I fall victim to enemies of my soul, break in the name of Jesus.

37. Every embargo placed upon me in the dark world to seal my mouth from prayer, break in the name of Jesus.

38. Every embargo assigned to seal my heaven, break in the name of Jesus.

39. O God of Elijah, shake heaven, shake earth, move me to my place of glory, in the name of Jesus

40. Breakthrough that will embarrass my household locate me in the name of Jesus

41. By the power of the living God, I will not die poor, in the name of Jesus

42. Every good thing I lost in the past I recover you , in the name of Jesus

43. O God of Elijah, open your treasure to me and bless me, in the name of Jesus

44. O God arise, give me testimony that will shake the world in the name of Jesus

45. Lord Jesus, overshadow my household in the name of Jesus.

CHAPTER 13

O LORD BREAK EMBARGO THAT COUNTER ANOINTING OF GOD

Numbers 12:1-2

1. Miriam and Aaron began to talk against Moses because of his Cushite wife, for he had married a Cushite.

2. "Has the LORD spoken only through Moses?" they asked. "Hasn't he also spoken through us?" And the LORD heard this.

1 Samuel 15:27-29

27. As Samuel turned to leave, Saul caught hold of the hem of his robe, and it tore.

28. Samuel said to him, "The LORD has torn the kingdom of Israel from you today and has given it to one of your neighborsto one better than you.

29. He who is the Glory of Israel does not lie or change his mind; for he is not a human being, that he should change his mind."

1. I thank you Lord, for the anointing you bless me with, in the name of Jesus
2. I thank you Lord, for your love and compassion, for my life, in the name of Jesus

3. O Lord, forgive me and strengthen me to see your face, in the name of Jesus

4. O Lord, let your forgiveness for my life, be permanent, in the name of Jesus

5. Holy Ghost Power, protect me for exploits in the name of Jesus

6. Holy Spirit, guide me from falling into pit of disgrace, in the name of Jesus.

7. Holy Ghost Power, pour fresh anointing of God upon me, in the name of Jesus

8. Blood of Jesus, flow in my life and multiply my anointing, in the name of Jesus

9. Blood of Jesus, miss with anointing of God for my life and miracles in the name of Jesus

10. I drink blood of Jesus, to revive and strengthen me for exploits, in the name of Jesus

11. Every embargo that counter anointing of God in my life, break and scatter, in the name of Jesus

12. I command every embargo assign to dry anointing of God on my head to scatter in the name of Jesus

13. I command every embargo assign to dry anointing of God on my career to scatter in the name of Jesus

14. I command every embargo assign to dry anointing of God on my calling to scatter in the name of Jesus

15. I command every embargo assign to dry anointing of God in my marriage to scatter, in the name of Jesus

16. Witchcraft embargo assign to dry anointing of success in my life, scatter in the name of Jesus

17. Satanic consultation aimed against anointing of God in my life, scatter in the name of Jesus

18. My anointing in the grip of marine power, I recover you by fire in the name of Jesus

19. Contrary anointing that wants me to weep instead of laugh, dry up in the name of Jesus

20. Every contrary spirit in charge of my destiny, die in the name of Jesus

21. Powers behind my fall, you shall fail, I will not fail or fall in the name of Jesus

22. Unrepentant stubborn pursuers after my life, run mad in name Of Jesus

23. Powers of my father's house after my life, die in the name of Jesus

24. Anti-clock wise spirit that place embargo upon my destiny die, in the name of Jesus

25. Powers of the night assign to counter my anointing, die in the name of Jesus

26. I command wicked powers and their embargoes to die, in the name of Jesus

27. Let the wisdom of the wicked become foolish any time they rise up against me in the name of Jesus

28. Embargo of darkness assign to break my jug of anointing break and scatter, in the name of Jesus.

29. Every contrary plea against my anointing scatter in the name of Jesus

30. Dark cloud around my anointing, clear away in the name of Jesus

31. Embargo that brings anguish, break in the name of Jesus

32. O Lord do not let me lose my anointing in your anger in the name of Jesus

33. Every satanic network build to tamper with my anointing, catch fire and roast to ashes, in the name of Jesus

34. Queen of heaven after my anointing, die in the name of Jesus

35. I command every evil program targeted against my anointing to scatter, in the name of Jesus

36. Every power behind my problem, die in the name of Jesus

37. Affliction of my father's house, troubling my anointing, die in the name of Jesus

38. Powers that sit on my anointing, be unseated in the name of Jesus

39. I command powers calling my name in witchcraft coven to die, in the name of Jesus

40. Anything buried, to bury my anointing , die in the name of Jesus

41. Powers assign to suck the honey of my anointing, die in the name of Jesus

42. Healing anointing in my life, manifest and explode, in the name of Jesus

43. Anointing that breaks the yoke, fall upon me in the name of Jesus

44. Anointing in my life become fire and consume every embargo on my way, in the name of Jesus

45. O Lord, release unto me anointing that shall not put me to shame, in the name of Jesus

46. O Lord, let anointing that break embargo of hopelessness come upon me, in the name of Jesus

47. O Lord, let anointing that dissolve and kill seed of hatred planted in my life, flow in my life, in the name of Jesus

48. Anointing that multiply favour of God in a life, flow in my life, in the name of Jesus

49. Anointing of surplus that multiply wealth, flow in my life in the name of Jesus

50. Henceforth, I command anointing of God to flow in my life twenty four hours every day, in the name of Jesus.

CHAPTER 14

O LORD BREAK EMBARGO AGAINST FAMILY GROWTH

Genesis 32:10-12

10. I am unworthy of all the kindness and faithfulness you have shown your servant. I had only my staff when I crossed this Jordan, but now I have become two camps.

11. Save me, I pray, from the hand of my brother Esau, for I am afraid he will come and attack me, and also the mothers with their children.

12. But you have said, 'I will surely make you prosper and will make your descendants like the sand of the sea, which cannot be counted.'"

Psalm 22:20-23

20. Deliver me from the sword, my precious life from the power of the dogs.

21. Rescue me from the mouth of the lions; save me from the horns of the wild oxen.

22. I will declare your name to my people; in the assembly I will praise you.

23. You who fear the LORD, praise him! All you descendants of Jacob, honor him! Revere him, all you descendants of Israel!

1. I thank you Lord, that you will empower me to defeat the Goliath against my family, in the name of Jesus

2. I thank you Lord for your protection upon my family, in the name of Jesus

3. O Lord, forgive my family every unrepentant sin troubling my lineage in the name of Jesus

4. O Lord, let your forgiveness for my family be permanent in the name of Jesus

5. Holy Spirit, guide my family to next level in the name of Jesus

6. Fire of God scatter every conspiracy against my family in the name of Jesus

7. I cover myself and family with blood of Jesus.

8. Blood of Jesus, block every flying route of witchcraft to my family, in the name of Jesus

9. O Lord, scatter every witchcraft design for my family in the name of Jesus

10. O Lord, tonight, reverse the battle, turn me to terror and dread of enemies troubling my family growth in the name of Jesus

11. I command every counsel against my family growth to expire in the name of Jesus

12. Wicked embargo as a result of evil counsel against my family, break in the name of Jesus

13. I command every embargo against my family growth to scatter, in the name of Jesus

14. I command every weapon of witchcraft against my family to catch fire and roast to ashes in the name of Jesus

15. Eaters of flesh and drinkers of blood in my family tormenting my immediate home, eat your flesh and drink your blood in the name of Jesus

16. Witchcraft load tormenting my family, catch fire and roast to ashes in the name of Jesus

17. Every embargo causing satanic re-arrangement in my family break and scatter in the name of Jesus

18. Any witchcraft power in my family compound retarding our progress, catch fire and roast to ashes, in the name of Jesus

19. Altar of witchcraft power in my family compound retarding our progress, catch fire and roast to ashes , in the name of Jesus

20. Witchcraft mark in my family house be erased by blood of Jesus

21. Witchcraft powers assign to exchange the glory of my family, die, in the name of Jesus

22. Any witchcraft power assign to exchange my glory die in the name of Jesus

23. Every embargo placed upon the foundation of my family, break in the name of Jesus

24. Every embargo upon my family as a result of any organ of my body taken to witchcraft coven, break in the name of Jesus

25. Every embargo placed upon my family as a result of my picture taken to witchcraft altar, break in the name of Jesus

26. Every embargo placed upon my family as a result of family picture taken to witchcraft altar, break in the name of Jesus

27. Every embargo place upon my family as a result of the picture of any member of my family to evil altar, break in the name of Jesus

28. Let God arise and scatter witchcraft plans organized against my family in the name of Jesus

29. Let every transportation means of witchcraft against my family catch fire and roast to ashes, in the name of Jesus

30. Every curse of witchcraft power that place embargo on my family break in the name of Jesus

31. I command every embargo upon my marriage to break in the name of Jesus

32. I command every embargo upon my children to break in the name of Jesus

33. Every witchcraft cage fashioned against my house, break in the name of Jesus

34. I command every coven of witchcraft fashion against my family to break in the name of Jesus
35. I command every covenant of witchcraft over my family to break in the name of Jesus
36. I command every witchcraft pattern fashion against my family to break in the name of Jesus
37. Inherited witchcraft troubling my family die in the name of Jesus
38. Dark powers, drawing power from the heavenly to torment my family die, In the name of Jesus
39. Every power waging war against my family die, in the name of Jesus
40. My family shall walk over every destiny demoting powers in the name of Jesus
41. Today, I raise altar of continuous prosperity for my family in the name of Jesus
42. Nobody shall die in my family for enemy to rejoice, in the name of Jesus
43. Today, I prophesy, my family shall be a crown of glory in the hand of God, in the name of Jesus
44. Lord Jesus, let your light shine upon my family in the name of Jesus
45. Henceforth, my God shall do exceeding abundance to me in the name of Jesus

CHAPTER 15

O LORD BREAK EMBARGO OF WITCHCRAFT CHAIN

Psalm 2:3

3. "Let us break their chains and throw off their shackles."

Psalm 30:9-10

9. "What is gained if I am silenced, if I go down to the pit? Will the dust praise you? Will it proclaim your faithfulness?

10. Hear, LORD, and be merciful to me; LORD, be my help."

1. I thank you Lord, for your protection upon my life, in the name of Jesus
2. I thank you Lord, for your love for me to break chain of darkness in my life, in the name of Jesus
3. Lord Jesus, forgive me, let the chains in my life break to pieces
4. Holy Spirit, work miracle in my life, in the name of Jesus
5. Holy Spirit, deliver me of evil chain in the name of Jesus

6. O God arise deliver me of evil chain, prepare for me by the enemy, in the name of Jesus

7. Blood of Jesus, break every witchcraft chain fashion against my breakthrough, in the name of Jesus.

8. I sprinkle blood of Jesus on wicked chains that hold me captive to break and scatter, in the name of Jesus

9. O Lord, in your anger rebuke enemies against my breakthrough, in the name of Jesus

10. O Lord, dash enemies of my soul to pieces like pottery, in the name of Jesus

11. Every embargo created so that I may not lift up my head, break in the name of Jesus

12. Embargo of anguish created so that I may not lift up my head, break in the name of Jesus

13. Chain of embargo in my hands break in the name of Jesus.

14. Every yoke on my shoulder, break in the name of Jesus.

15. Feathers of darkness in my hands, holding me captive, break, in the name of Jesus.

16. Every trouble assign for me in the spirit, die in the name of Jesus.

17. Evil padlock fashioned against my destiny, break in the name of Jesus.

18. Finger of God touch and break evil chain that held me captive, in the name of Jesus.
19. Evil calendar of darkness monitoring evil chain in my life, catch fire and roast to ashes, in the name of Jesus.
20. Star killers using dark chain to torment me, die in the name of Jesus.
21. Altar of darkness backing up poverty in my life, catch fire and roast to ashes, in the name of Jesus.
22. Every embargo as a result of witchcraft rope used to tie me down in the spirit, break in the name of Jesus.
23. Every chain in my leg as a result of evil embargo, break in the name of Jesus.
24. Every chain in my hands as a result of witchcraft embargo, break in the name of Jesus.
25. Every chain in my waist as a result of witchcraft embargo, break in the name of Jesus.
26. O Lord, break the teeth of the wicked that lay wicked embargo upon me, in the name of Jesus.
27. Evil storm in my life as a result of dark chain in my life, scatter in the name of Jesus.
28. Those that boast, God shall not deliver me, shall fail, in the name of Jesus.
29. Chain of darkness in my life, attracting evil, break in the name of Jesus.

30. Satanic ammunition prepared to destroy me, catch fire and roast to ashes, in the name of Jesus.
31. Every source of affliction in my life, dry up in the name of Jesus.
32. Deadly trap with evil chain set to catch me, break to pieces and catch fire in the name of Jesus.
33. I shall breakthrough and not breakdown in the name of Jesus.
34. Wicked embargo, assign to swallow my wealth and riches break in the name of Jesus.
35. Every yoke in my life, break in the name of Jesus.
36. Blood of Jesus, break evil chain that tied me down, in the name of Jesus.
37. Light of God shall shine upon me and break chains of darkness in my life, in the name of Jesus.
38. Fear of the wicked around me, expire in the name of Jesus.
39. I command thunder fire of God to scatter every dark power drawn up against me, in the name of Jesus.
40. O Lord, strike my enemies on the jaw and make them bow in shame in the name of Jesus.

41. I bind and cast out demons in my hands, in the name of Jesus.
42. O Lord, let my presence command authority wherever I go, in the name of Jesus.
43. I anoint my hands with anointing of breakthrough, in the name of Jesus.
44. By the power of the living God, as many as they that rise against me shall scatter, in the name of Jesus.
45. I praise God who is always there for me, in the name of Jesus.

CHAPTER 16

O LORD BREAK EMBARGO PLACED UPON MY LAUGHTER AND JOY

Numbers 22:12

12. But God said to Balaam, "Do not go with them. You must not put a curse on those people, because they are blessed."

Psalm 20:4-8

4. May he give you the desire of your heart and make all your plans succeed.

5. May we shout for joy over your victory and lift up our banners in the name of our God. May the LORD grant all your requests.

6. Now this I know: The LORD gives victory to his anointed. He answers him from his heavenly sanctuary with the victorious power of his right hand.

7. Some trust in chariots and some in horses, but we trust in the name of the LORD our God.

8. They are brought to their knees and fall, but we rise up and stand firm.

1. I thank you O Lord, for the joy and laughter you bless me with, in the name of Jesus.

2. Lord Jesus, thank you for your mercy upon me.

3. Lord Jesus, erase love for sin in my life, in the name of Jesus.

4. Lord Jesus, forgive me, do not rebuke me in your anger, in the name of Jesus.

5. Be merciful to me O Lord, break every embargo of darkness troubling my life, in the name of Jesus.

6. Holy Spirit, fill me afresh, in the name of Jesus.

7. Holy Spirit, sanitize my mouth to speak breakthrough and joy to my life, in the name of Jesus.

8. O Lord, let my prayer draw you close to me and me to you, in the name of Jesus.

9. Powers assign to defile me in the spirit, die, in the name of Jesus.

10. Lord Jesus, catapult my spiritual life to great height, in the name of Jesus.

11. Every embargo placed on me to miss my way, break in the name of Jesus.

12. Any power assign to scatter the glory of God in my life, die in the name of Jesus.

13. Every embargo upon my life break, let my harvest start now in the name of Jesus.

14. Every negative pronouncement against my breakthrough, be nullified, break, in the name of Jesus.

15. Every wicked arrangement to place embargo upon my career, scatter and break in the name of Jesus.
16. Every embargo arranged to make God frown at me, break and scatter, in the name of Jesus.
17. Every embargo that bring destruction to life assign for me, break and scatter in the name of Jesus.
18. Every yoke upon my life, scatter in the name of Jesus.
19. Blood of Jesus, break every embargo upon my life, in the name of Jesus.
20. Every embargo that will make me careless with my career, break in the name of Jesus.
21. Dark embargo assigned to place me in wilderness of life, break in the name of Jesus.
22. Every embargo placed on me, to harvest poverty as food, break in the name of Jesus.
23. Every barrier around me, break and scatter, in the name of Jesus.
24. Every embargo that attracts forces of darkness to my life, break in the name of Jesus.
25. Dark embargo that distance me from favour of God, break in the name of Jesus.
26. Every embargo that attracts cloud of darkness to my life, break in the name of Jesus.

27. Hammer of God, break every embargo of stagnancy placed upon me, in the name of Jesus.

28. Every embargo placed on me to fall in every step I take, break in the name of Jesus.

29. Every embargo placed on me that assign powers from pit of hell to kill me, break, in the name of Jesus.

30. Wicked personalities on assignment to pull me down, die, in the name of Jesus.

31. Broom of God, sweep enemies on my way to breakthrough, in the name of Jesus.

32. Purse with holes, in my life, be sealed with blood of Jesus.

33. Any power occupying my seat of glory be unseated, in the name of Jesus.

34. O Lord my God, kill spirit of arrogance in my life, in the name of Jesus.

35. By the power that demote Vatshi and promote Esther, I occupy my divine destiny, in the name of Jesus.

36. My career, receive heavenly blessing in the name of Jesus.

37. O Lord, anoint my head with fresh oil, in the name of Jesus.

38. Honey of God, overflow and bless my handwork in the name of Jesus.

39. Every embargo of household wickedness upon my life, break, in the name of Jesus.
40. I receive anointing to overtake and excel in what I do, in the name of Jesus.
41. My finance receive heavenly blessing, in the name of Jesus.
42. O Lord, enlarge my coast beyond my expectation, in the name of Jesus.
43. Today is my day, I am a conqueror who flies from sky of rejection to the firmament of dominion, in the name of Jesus.
44. Today is my day, I swim from river of pain to river of breakthrough, in the name of Jesus.
45. O Lord, let me dig the well of my prosperity, and have it, in the name of Jesus.

YOU HAVE BATTLES TO WIN
TRY THESE BOOKS
1. COMMAND THE DAY.

Each day of the week is loaded with meanings and divine assurance. God did not create each day of the week for the fun of it. Blessings, success, gifts, resources, hopes, portfolios, duties, rights, prophecies, warnings and challenges, are loaded in each day.

Do you know the language, command or decree you can use to claim what belongs to you in each day of the week? Do you know in Christendom, Monday can be equated to one of the days of creation in Genesis chapter one? Do you know creation lasted for six days and God rested on the seventh day? What day of the week can Christian equate as the first day of the week, if we follow Christian calendar? What day can we call day seven?

This book shall give insight to these questions. It shall explain how you can command each day of the week according to creation in the book of Genesis chapter one.

Above all, you shall exercise your right and claim what is hidden in each day of the week.
Check for this in **COMMAND THE DAY.**

2. PRAYER TO REMEMBER DREAMS

A lot of people are passing through this spiritual epidemic on a daily basis. Their dream life is epileptic, having no ability to remember all dreams they dream, or sometimes forget everything entirely. This is nothing but spiritual havoc you need to erase from your spiritual record.

The answer to every form of spiritual blackout caused by spiritual erasers is found in, **PRAYER TO REMEMBER DREAMS.**

3.100% CONFESSSIONS AND PROPHECIES TO LOCATE HELPERS.

This is a wonderful book on confessions and prophecies to locate helpers and helpers to locate you. It is a prayer book loaded with over two thousand (2,000) prayer points.

The book unravels how to locate unknown helpers, prayers to arrest mind of helpers and prayers for manifestation after encounter with helpers.

4. ANOINTING FOR ELEVENTH HOUR HELP.

This book tells much of what to do at injury hour called eleventh hour. When you read and use this book as prescribed fear shall vanish in your life when pursuing a project, career or contract.

5. PRAYER TO LOCATE HELPERS.

Our divine helper is God. He created us to be together and be of help to one another. In the midst of no help we lost out, ending our journey in the wilderness.

There are keys assign to open right doors of life. You need right key to locate your helpers. Enough is enough; of suffering in silence.

With this book, you shall locate your helpers while your helpers shall locate you.

6. FIRE FOR FIRE PRAYER BOOK

This prayer book is fast at answering spiritual problems. It is a bulldozer prayer book, full of prayers all through. It is highly recommended for night vigil. Testimonies are pouring in daily from users of this book across the world!

7. PRAYER FOR THE FRUIT OF THE WOMB

This prayer book is children magnet. By faith and believe in God Almighty, as soon as you use this book open doors to child bearing shall be yours. Amen

8. PRAYER FOR PREGNANT WOMEN.

This is a spiritual prayer book loaded with prayers of solution for pregnant women. As soon as you take in, the prayers you shall pray from day one of conception to the day of delivery are written in this book.

9. WARFARE IN THE OFFICE

It is high time you pray prayers of power must change hands in office. Use this book and liberate yourself from every form of office yoke.

10. MY MARRIAGE SHALL NOT BREAK

Marriage is corner piece of life, happiness and joy. You need to hold it tight and guide it from wicked intruders and destroyer of homes.

11. VICTORY OVER SATANIC HOUSE 1 & 2

Are you a tenant, Land lord bombarded left and right, front and back by wicked people around you?

With this book you shall be liberated from the hooks of the enemy.

12. DICTIONARY OF DREAMS

This is a must book for every home. It gives accurate details to about **10,000 (Ten thousand) dreams and interpretations,** written in alphabetical order for quick reference and easy digestion. The book portrays spiritual revelations

with sound prophetic guidelines. It is loaded with Biblical references and violent prayers.
Ask for yours today.

For Further Enquiries Contact
THE AUTHOR
EVANGELIST TELLA OLAYERI
P.O. Box 1872 Shomolu Lagos.
Tel: 08023583168

FROM AUTHOR'S DESK

BEFORE YOU GO

Hello,

Thank you for purchasing this book. Would you consider posting a review about this book? In addition to providing feedback and arousing others into Christ's bosom, reviews can help other customers to know about the book.

Please take a minute to leave a review on this book.

I would appreciate that!

Thank you in advance, for your review and your patronage!!

NOTE: You can get all my books from my website www.tellaolayeri.com

GOOD NEWS!!!

My audiobook is now available, to get one visit acx.com and search **"Tella Olayeri."**

Brethren, to be loaded and reloaded visit: *amazon.com/author/tellaolayeri* for a full spiritual sojourn for my books.

Thanks.